Francis Frith's

Essex

Photographic Memories

Francis Frith's
Essex

Helen Livingston

First published in the United Kingdom in 2000 by
The Francis Frith Collection

Hardback Edition 2000
ISBN 1-85937-082-9

Paperback Edition 2000
ISBN 1-85937-270-8

Reprinted in Paperback 2001 & 2003

British Library Cataloguing in Publication Data

Francis Frith's Essex
Helen Livingston

The Francis Frith Collection
Frith's Barn, Teffont,
Salisbury, Wiltshire SP3 5QP
Tel: +44 (0) 1722 716 376
Email: info@francisfrith.co.uk
www.francisfrith.com

Printed and bound in Great Britain

Front Cover: **CHELMSFORD, HIGH STREET 1895** 35514T

AS WITH ANY HISTORICAL DATABASE THE FRITH ARCHIVE IS CONSTANTLY BEING CORRECTED AND IMPROVED AND THE PUBLISHERS WOULD WELCOME INFORMATION ON OMISSIONS OR INACCURACIES

Contents

FRANCIS FRITH: *Victorian Pioneer*

FRANCIS FRITH, Victorian founder of the world-famous photographic archive, was a complex and multitudinous man. A devout Quaker and a highly successful Victorian businessman, he was both philosophic by nature and pioneering in outlook.

By 1855 Francis Frith had already established a wholesale grocery business in Liverpool, and sold it for the astonishing sum of £200,000, which is the equivalent today of over £15,000,000. Now a multi-millionaire, he was able to indulge his passion for travel. As a child he had pored over travel books written by early explorers, and his fancy and imagination had been stirred by family holidays to the sublime mountain regions of Wales and Scotland. 'What a land of spirit-stirring and enriching scenes and places!' he had written. He was to return to these scenes of grandeur in later years to 'recapture the thousands of vivid and tender memories', but with a different purpose. Now in his thirties, and captivated by the new science of photography, Frith set out on a series of pioneering journeys to the Nile regions that occupied him from 1856 until 1860.

INTRIGUE AND ADVENTURE

He took with him on his travels a specially-designed wicker carriage that acted as both dark-room and sleeping chamber. These far-flung journeys were packed with intrigue and adventure. In his life story, written when he was sixty-three, Frith tells of being held captive by bandits, and of fighting 'an awful midnight battle to the very point of surrender with a deadly pack of hungry, wild dogs'. Sporting flowing Arab costume, Frith arrived at Akaba by camel seventy years before Lawrence, where he encountered 'desert princes and rival sheikhs, blazing with jewel-hilted swords'.

During these extraordinary adventures he was assiduously exploring the desert regions bordering the Nile and patiently recording the antiquities and peoples with his camera. He was the first photographer to venture beyond the sixth cataract. Africa was still the mysterious 'Dark Continent', and Stanley and Livingstone's historic meeting was a decade into the future. The conditions for picture taking confound belief. He laboured for hours in his wicker darkroom in the sweltering heat of the desert, while the volatile chemicals fizzed dangerously in their trays. Often he was forced to work in remote tombs and caves where conditions were cooler. Back in London he exhibited his photographs and was 'rapturously cheered' by members of the Royal Society. His reputation as a photographer was made overnight. An eminent modern historian has likened their impact on the population of the time to that on our own generation of the first photographs taken on the surface of the moon.

VENTURE OF A LIFE-TIME

Characteristically, Frith quickly spotted the opportunity to create a new business as a specialist publisher of photographs. He lived in an era of immense and sometimes violent change. For the poor in the early part of Victoria's reign work was a drudge and the hours long, and people had precious little free time to enjoy themselves. Most had no transport other than a cart or gig at their disposal, and had not travelled far beyond the boundaries of their own town or village. However, by the 1870s, the railways had threaded their way across the country, and Bank Holidays and half-day Saturdays had been made obligatory by Act of Parliament. All of a sudden the ordinary working man and his family were able to enjoy days out and see a little more of the world.

With characteristic business acumen, Francis Frith foresaw that these new tourists would enjoy having souvenirs to commemorate their days out. In 1860 he married Mary Ann Rosling and set out with the intention of photographing every city, town and village in Britain. For the next thirty years he travelled the country by train and by pony and trap, producing fine photographs of seaside resorts and beauty spots that were keenly bought by millions of Victorians. These prints were painstakingly pasted into family albums and pored over during the dark nights of winter, rekindling precious memories of summer excursions.

THE RISE OF FRITH & CO

Frith's studio was soon supplying retail shops all over the country. To meet the demand he gathered about him a small team of photographers, and published the work of independent artist-photographers of the calibre of Roger Fenton and Francis Bedford. In order to gain some understanding of the scale of Frith's business one only has to look at the catalogue issued by Frith & Co in 1886: it runs to some 670 pages, listing not only many thousands

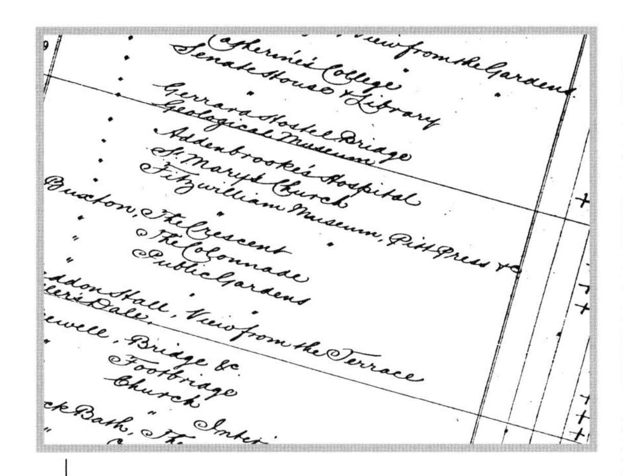

Senate House & Library
Gerrard Hostel Bridge
Geological Museum
Addenbrooke's Hospital
St. Mary's Church
Fitzwilliam Museum, Pitt Press
The Crescent
The Colonnade
Public Gardens
View from the Terrace
Bridge &c.
Footbridge
Church

of views of the British Isles but also many photographs of most European countries, and China, Japan, the USA and Canada – note the sample page shown above from the hand-written *Frith & Co* ledgers detailing pictures taken. By 1890 Frith had created the greatest specialist photographic publishing company in the world, with over 2,000 outlets – more than the combined number that Boots and WH Smith have today! The picture on the right shows the *Frith & Co* display board at Ingleton in the Yorkshire Dales. Beautifully constructed with mahogany frame and gilt inserts, it could display up to a dozen local scenes.

Postcard Bonanza

The ever-popular holiday postcard we know today took many years to develop. In 1870 the Post Office issued the first plain cards, with a pre-printed stamp on one face. In 1894 they allowed other publishers' cards to be sent through the mail with an attached adhesive halfpenny stamp. Demand grew rapidly, and in 1895 a new size of postcard was permitted called the court card, but there was little room for illustration. In 1899, a year after Frith's death, a new card measuring 5.5 x 3.5 inches became the standard format, but it was not until 1902 that the divided back came into being, with address and message on one face and a full-size illustration on the other. *Frith & Co* were in the vanguard of postcard development, and Frith's sons Eustace and Cyril continued their father's monumental task, expanding the number of views offered to the public and recording more and more places in Britain, as the coasts and countryside were opened up to mass travel.

Francis Frith died in 1898 at his villa in Cannes, his great project still growing. The archive he created continued in business for another seventy years. By 1970 it contained over a third of a million pictures of 7,000 cities, towns and villages. The massive photographic record Frith has left to us stands as a living monument to a special and very remarkable man.

Frith's Archive: *A Unique Legacy*

Francis Frith's legacy to us today is of immense significance and value, for the magnificent archive of evocative photographs he created provides a unique record of change in 7,000 cities, towns and villages throughout Britain over a century and more. Frith and his fellow studio photographers revisited locations many times down the years to update their views, compiling for us an enthralling and colourful pageant of British life and character.

We tend to think of Frith's sepia views of Britain as nostalgic, for most of us use them to conjure up memories of places in our own lives with which we have family associations. It often makes us forget that to Francis Frith they were records of daily life as it was actually being lived in the cities, towns and villages of his day. The Victorian age was one of great and often bewildering change for ordinary people, and though the pictures evoke an impression of slower times, life was as busy and hectic as it is today.

We are fortunate that Frith was a photographer of the people, dedicated to recording the minutiae of everyday life. For it is this sheer wealth of visual data, the painstaking chronicle of changes in dress, transport, street layouts, buildings, housing, engineering and landscape that captivates us so much today. His remarkable images offer us a powerful link with the past and with the lives of our ancestors.

See Frith at www.francisfrith.co.uk

Today's Technology

Computers have now made it possible for Frith's many thousands of images to be accessed almost instantly. In the Frith archive today, each photograph is carefully 'digitised' then stored on a CD Rom. Frith archivists can locate a single photograph amongst thousands within seconds. Views can be catalogued and sorted under a variety of categories of place and content to the immediate benefit of researchers. Inexpensive reference prints can be created for them at the touch of a mouse button, and a wide range of books and other printed materials assembled and published for a wider, more general readership, The day-to-day workings of the archive are very different from how they were in Francis

Frith's time: imagine the herculean task of sorting through eleven tons of glass negatives as Frith had to do to locate a particular sequence of pictures! Yet the archive still prides itself on maintaining the same high standards of excellence laid down by Francis Frith, including the painstaking cataloguing and indexing of every view.

It is curious to reflect on how the internet now allows researchers in America and elsewhere greater instant access to the archive than Frith himself ever enjoyed. Many thousands of individual views can be called up on screen within seconds on one of the Frith internet sites, enabling people living continents away to revisit the streets of their ancestral home town, or view places in Britain where they have enjoyed holidays. Many overseas researchers welcome the chance to view special theme selections, such as transport, sports, costume and ancient monuments.

We are certain that Francis Frith would have heartily approved of these modern developments, for he himself was always working at the very limits of Victorian photographic technology.

The Value of the Archive Today

Because of the benefits brought by the computer, Frith's images are increasingly studied by social historians, by researchers into genealogy and ancestory, by architects, town planners, and by teachers and schoolchildren involved in local history projects. In addition, the archive offers every one of us a unique opportunity to examine the places where we and our families have lived and worked down the years. Immensely successful in Frith's own era, the archive is now, a century and more on, entering a new phase of popularity.

The Past in Tune with the Future

Historians consider the Francis Frith Collection to be of prime national importance. It is the only archive of its kind remaining in private ownership and has been valued at a million pounds. However, this figure is now rapidly increasing as digital technology enables more and more people around the world to enjoy its benefits.

Francis Frith's archive is now housed in an historic timber barn in the beautiful village of Teffont in Wiltshire. Its founder would not recognize the archive office as it is today. In place of the many thousands of dusty boxes containing glass plate negatives and an all-pervading odour of photographic chemicals, there are now ranks of computer screens. He would be amazed to watch his images travelling round the world at unimaginable speeds through network and internet lines.

The archive's future is both bright and exciting. Francis Frith, with his unshakeable belief in making photographs available to the greatest number of people, would undoubtedly approve of what is being done today with his lifetime's work. His photographs, depicting our shared past, are now bringing pleasure and enlightenment to millions around the world a century and more after his death.

Essex – *An Introduction*

Essex has for so long been the poor relation of the home counties that its long and noble history appears to have almost slipped from memory. It is a county considered by many to be industrial, built over and impoverished. It is a 'music hall joke' of a county, and this has been so for generations. 'Essex?' folk have said for at least a century - 'flat', 'boring', 'mud-fringed', 'a London suburb'. But how untrue! These photos tell quite another story.

Essex above all English counties presents so many different faces to the world as to be several counties rolled into one. To the outsider it is difficult indeed to classify Essex. This is a big square county, covering some 978,000 acres, one of the biggest in England, and it includes a vast variety of 'landscapes' within its borders. To a great extent these still follow their ancient delineations: the Thames estuary to the south, the North Sea coast to the east, the Rivers Lea and Stort to the west and the River Stour -Constable's River Stour, much painted by the famous artist - on the north.

Those who know Essex also know that those who castigate her as 'flat' or 'boring' or as a kind of London-squatter-land have probably never ventured far across the county boundary. They also know that this lack of interest is in a way Essex's gain. The county remains largely unspoiled. Beyond its south-west fringe and the industrial-cum-honky-tonk part of Thames-side, Essex is a land of small towns, of widely-spaced villages and tiny hamlets that have seen little change, one feels, since the conqueror. Many of the century-old scenes pictured in this book are immediately recognisable and little changed. A glance at a map of Essex shows a settlement pattern that has vanished forever from the better known 'home counties', and even today the visitor has the sensation of revisiting an earlier age along the byways.

The landscape is not generally flat; it includes the rolling hills along the Suffolk border, while in the south of the county such little eminences as Danbury (380 feet) and Laindon (387 feet) rise from the surrounding undulating land with such abruptness as to appear far more lofty than many a great hill elsewhere. This is English farmland at its best, a satisfying rural scene with clumps of trees, small woodlands and individual oaks and ashes breaking the view presided over by the hurrying skies. Trees dominate the scene in Epping Forest, the majestic remnant of the once spacious royal forest of Essex, established in Norman times. Beyond the countryside and the woodlands are the towns, not only the bustling New Towns within London's orbit, but noisy seaside resorts like Southend and Clacton, the international port of Harwich, and also ancient foundations. The county town, Chelmsford, dates from the time of the Romans, but in terms of antiquarian interest it is overshadowed by the venerable town of Colchester - a town before the Romans made it their first British capital. Lastly, there is remote Essex, the marshes and creeks of the south east, the region around the rivers Crouch and Blackwater, where sinuous tideways finger far inland under the huge dome of the sky, and break up the land, making the whole area difficult of access save by boat.

Essex is an ancient county with a recorded history that pre-dates the successful Roman invasion of AD43. In those days it was home to the Trinovantes, probably the most powerful British Celtic 'tribe', under their king, Cunobelinus (Shakespeare's Cymbeline). Their main town was at Colchester, and it was to Colchester, the Roman Camulodunum, that the Emperor Claudius hurried with his army to receive the tribute of twelve British kings and declare Britain a Roman province with its capital at Colchester. A temple was built there to the deified Claudius; its foundations remain under the Norman Colchester Castle, but it was burned to the ground in Boudicca's rebellion of AD 60, along with those who has taken refuge there. Soon after this, London displaced Colchester as capital and hub of the road network, though Colchester remained an important Roman town.

With the collapse of Roman rule Essex was in the forefront of the Saxon colonisation, and a Saxon kingdom was set up. The county's name dates from this time - the land of the East Saxons - but in AD991 the Saxons were defeated by the Danes in the disastrous Battle of Maldon, a battle well-known on account of the fine Anglo-Saxon poem written about it not long after the event. A further Saxon defeat took place at the Battle of Assundun

(probably Ashingdon, near Wickford) in 1016, when the 23-year-old Dane, Cnut (Canute), defeated the Saxon king, Edmund Ironside, and established himself as king.

During Saxon times, Christianity had been brought to eastern Essex by St Cedd, who built the little church at Bradwell on the site of the former Roman fort of Othona. Once

the Danes had been converted, monastic establishments flourished, none more so than at Waltham Abbey, founded by Cnut's standard bearer, Tovi.

Under the Normans a number of important castles were built in the county. The most magnificent is certainly Colchester Castle, built by a supporter of William Rufus who was granted Colchester by a grateful king. It is the biggest Norman keep ever built, either here or in France, and was once a bulky four storeys high. It served for years as a prison, and is now a museum. The edifice at Castle Headingham was built during King Stephen's reign, while the now very ruinous Hadleigh Castle overlooking the Thames estuary, and famous for Constable's painting of it, was built by Edward III against a possible French invasion. It succumbed not to bombardment but to land subsidence; it is pictured in this book prior to the development of the eponymous country park. Other Norman castles include the famous Pleshey, between Chelmsford and Dunmow.

The Middle Ages and the Tudor era saw parts of Essex, notably the northern half, wax prosperous on agriculture. Big churches were built - as they were in neighbouring Suffolk - and some splendid timber 'guild houses' remain - notably that at Thaxted, which is pictured here before traffic took over the little town. Saffron Walden built its pleasing square on the proceeds of saffron bulb production. The saffron crocus was thought to have remarkable medicinal properties as well as its now better-known uses for dyeing cloth and in cookery.

Other parts of the county remained poor, particularly along the creeks and inlets of the south-east, where fishing remained the important stay and smuggling was endemic. Some fishing villages, notably Brightlingsea, had famous oyster beds - the Brightlingsea beds supplied the fare for the annual Colchester Oyster Feast, which still takes place every October.

The turnpike era benefited from the legacy of the Romans, and many of their superb Essex roads were adapted for coaching traffic. The Great Road from London to Colchester was turnpiked as the Great Essex Turnpike, and several old inns along it are featured in these pictures, notably at Witham.

The Victorian age, the later years of which feature in many of these pictures, was basically an age of quiet prosperity for the county. Its agriculture thrived. Its Thames-side industries developed. Change arrived with the railways, which allowed the development of the coastal resorts, an important feature of the late 19th and early 20th centuries. Several of these pictures show the development of hugely popular Southend, of boisterous Clacton, select Frinton and of Walton on the Naze.

Along the Thames estuary were several industrial developments which increased in importance as the years went by. Brick making, employing the fine 'brick earth' around Grays, was an important industry that helped build Victorian London, but recently has been unable to compete with mass-produced products. The chalk outcrops along the estuary near Purfleet were formerly quarried for agricultural lime and 'whiting', but later produced quantities of cement.

None the less, Essex has always been primarily an agricultural county, and its proximity to London certainly proved advantageous. Wheat was and still is a major crop, though today there is also a big acreage of sunflowers and oilseed rape. Until the late 19th century Essex livestock was driven to London on the hoof. Market gardens developed, particularly along the River Lea, once famed for its glasshouses. Another important Essex industry was the commercial production of seeds. Many famous varieties were first developed in the county - take, for instance, the Kelvedon Wonder pea.

The rich Essex farmland, famed for its wheat, and the many rivers, creeks and tidal inlets, combined to make ideal locations for big corn mills. Several are pictured here. These are no local mills, catering for the immediate community, but industrial-scale establishments. Some were ordinary water mills, but many were tide mills. The grain and flour were transported, as were other Essex commodities - bricks, hay and lime, to name but three - by the Thames sailing barge. There are several types of these superb flat-bottomed boats with their big tan sails (the 'spritty' - spritsail barges - and the 'stumpie' for example), but all were excellent workhorses which were generally worked along the creeks and rivers and along the coast to the Thames estuary. They were extremely seaworthy: many made regular North Sea or Channel crossings. Part of the fleet has been converted to pleasure use and is based at Maldon. Races are keenly contested, just as they were in the barges' working days.

Since the Second World War, the population of Essex has grown. Also, London has annexed the southern fringes. In some places, for example the New Towns of Harlow and Basildon, growth has been explosive. However, in many other parts of the county, particularly the rural fringe in the north, little growth has occurred. The county here is still predominantly rural, the landscape little changed since medieval times, in contrast to the other hard-pressed Home Counties.`

AVELEY, HIGH STREET c1955 A110002

Aveley is a small village situated a few miles to the east of Rainham and close to the Thames and Essex Marshes. The parked bicycles on the right, no cars to be seen and the crowd waiting for the bus speak of a vanished era. The village is now a stone's throw from the M25 and the new Queen Elizabeth II Bridge, shattering the former peace.

GRAYS, THE MARKET 1964 G85059

It is all bustle at the Market in this picture of the large Thames-side town, properly called Grays Thurrock. Grays was famous for its bricks, produced in quantity until recent times, from the fine wind-blown 'brick-earth' of the Thames Estuary.

TILBURY, DOCK ROAD c1960 T114005
Tilbury Docks - the lowest on the Thames - opened in 1886. They are now one of the largest container ports in Europe. The town developed to serve the docks; in this picture a group of dockers are seen heading to work.

TILBURY, THE THAMES c1960 T114009
There is an excellent view of the shipping on the Thames at Tilbury near the Ferry terminal. This picture is of a typical small cargo boat of the time, the Dutch 'Vruburgh'. Cargo boats such as this have been superseded by the rise of the container ship.

TILBURY, THE FERRY c1960 T114027
The Tilbury to Gravesend ferry still runs; it is one of the oldest-established ferries in south-east England. It was originally known just as the 'Cross Ferry' to distinguish it from the 'Long Ferry' that plied the 20 miles or so between Gravesend and London.

HORNDON ON THE HILL, HIGH STREET c1960 H178009
This hilltop village, a few miles to the south of Basildon, is known for its attractive architecture and ancient church. A society now promotes the preservation and appreciation of the compact village. The Bell Inn has unusual decor - every year since 1901 a fresh hot cross bun has been nailed to the rafters!

STANFORD LE HOPE, THE STATION c1955 S258314
A view of the station, taken about one hundred years after the line opened between Tilbury and Southend. All Southend trains came this way until the early 1880s, when the direct line from Southend to London via Basildon and Upminster was opened. Although by-passed, this line remained busy and was electrified in 1962.

CORRINGHAM, CHURCH ROAD c1955 C243023
An evocative view of old Corringham, down on the flat land close to the Thames and now a close neighbour to the estates of Thurrock and the Thames-side oil storage depots. In this picture timber weatherboarding, brick and tile combine to give an air of ancient peace.

CORRINGHAM, LAMPITS c1955 C243041
This view makes a rather sharp contrast with the above photograph; only the old man on his bike, walking stick on the front handlebars, gives this scene any rural charm. This is modern Corringham, in the heart of suburban Essex near the Thames.

CANVEY ISLAND, THE BEACH c1965 C237084
This low-lying island in the Thames estuary may have been the 'Conties' described by Ptolemy in his 'Geography'. Canvey Island has been a great Thames-side attraction for many years, though now the sea walls have been raised to protect the low-lying island in the event of the closing of the Thames Barrier.

HADLEIGH, THE CASTLE c1955 H167008
The ruinous towers of Hadleigh Castle were pictured by John Constable in a painting which he first exhibited in 1826. The Castle was originally built in 1232, and was rebuilt in 1365 against a possible French invasion. It is now an English Heritage property in the Hadleigh Castle Country Park.

HADLEIGH, RECTORY ROAD c1960 H167018
In complete contrast to photograph H167008, here we have a rainy morning in downtown Hadleigh by the Rectory Road shops. A pram is parked outside the butcher's shop, whilst on the opposite side of the road outside the Post Office two ladies are deep in conversation.

LEIGH-ON-SEA, STREET SCENE 1891 29066
Leigh-on-Sea is high on the hill overlooking the Thames Estuary, just west of Southend. The area has been built up considerably since this picture was taken, but attractive villas still descend the hill towards the sandy estuary, the railway and the pleasant shopping street.

PRITTLEWELL, THE VILLAGE 1891 29074

This was the original Southend. Prittlewell village existed in the Middle Ages; its 'south end', a group of fishermen's huts on the Thames Estuary, has grown to be the bustling town and seaside resort of that name today.

SOUTHEND, ON THE CLIFFS 1891 29048

Southend, the famous Thames estuary seaside resort, was developed from the late 18th century onwards. Originally it was a few fishermen's huts at the end of a lane south of Prittlewell. The cliffs shown here have since been further developed.

SOUTHEND, PIER HILL BUILDINGS 1898 40909

The Royal Hotel, seen in the background of this picture, was developed along with Royal Terrace between 1791 and 1793. In the foreground are Pier Hill Buildings, completed the year this photograph was taken. They were demolished in 1977.

SOUTHEND, THE BEACH 1898 40911
The central beach in the last years of the 19th century. Southend has seven miles of 'front'. The old pier is visible on the left.

SOUTHEND, FROM THE PIER 1898 41378
This view looks back to Southend from the pier over a century ago. Southend's popularity was greatly increased when the railway arrived in 1856. By 1906 locals were even suggesting it should change its name to 'Thamesmouth', reflecting its higher status. However, it remained plain old Southend.

SOUTHEND, THE PIER 1898 41377
Southend pier is the longest in the world - reaching out one and a quarter miles (2 kms) into the Thames estuary. It was originally built in wood in 1859, but it was extended and rebuilt in late Victorian times. An electric railway runs its entire length.

SOUTHEND, FROM THE PIER 1898 41382

Pleasure boats have lined up to collect trippers for the obligatory sail down the estuary. The picture was taken from the pier. The seafront architecture has changed little - but the shop blinds have vanished to make way for amusement arcades.

SOUTHEND, THE PIER c1960 S155085

The triumphal entrance to the longest pier in the world; the pier head is visible in the distance about a mile and a quarter away. The first pier was a wooden structure, but was rebuilt in iron after the local authority purchased it in 1875. A banner advertises a free 'Focus on America' exhibition at the Pier Head.

SOUTHEND, THE GOLDEN HIND C1955 S155039
A replica of the Golden Hind was exhibited for a time by the entrance to the Pier. Curious holidaymakers could tour the ship for the princely sum of 6d. A modern-day crew member is eyeing the photographer suspiciously.

SOUTHEND, THE AIRPORT C1960 S155154
The airport lies north of the town, close to Rochford. This evocative photograph, taken some forty years ago, shows passengers boarding an early jet aircraft near the terminal.

GREAT WAKERING, HIGH STREET c1955 G100002
Great Wakering is an attractive village, just a few miles to the north of Shoeburyness in the remote old marshlands of the south east of Essex. It stands above a wide stretch of the Maplin Sands and the fingering estuarine channels of the River Roach. This view looks along the quiet High Street.

SHOEBURYNESS, WEST BEACH c1955 S275007
An evocative view of the seaside, with deckchairs and pleasure craft on this low headland jutting out into the Thames estuary towards Kent. The coast swings away westwards along the Southend front.

ROCHFORD, MARKET SQUARE c1955 R226015
Rochford is a small town on the River Roach in south east Essex, a few miles to the north of Southend. The pleasing Market Square, pictured here, held its last cattle market in 1959, a few years after this picture was taken. The town may have been the birthplace of Anne Boleyn in about 1504.

ROCHFORD, STAMBRIDGE MILL c1955 R226016
The Mill stood to the south of Rochford on the tidal estuary of the River Roach. Many mills existed along the tidal arms of the sea fingering into Essex which provided easy transport by water. It was originally a water mill, and was owned by Rankins the Millers when it burned down in April 1965.

RAYLEIGH, THE VILLAGE 1951 R224018

Situated between Basildon and Southend and the estuaries of the rivers Thames and Crouch, Rayleigh is an ancient place that once sported a Norman Castle. The mound still stands, known as Rayleigh Mount, and now belongs to the National Trust.

RAYLEIGH, TOWN CENTRE 1957 R224027

The big 15th-century church of the Holy Trinity dominates this view of the town centre. The church contains Roman tiles re-used by the original Norman builders. Rayleigh still keeps its 'small town' feel despite surrounding developments.

WICKFORD, THE RIVER AT BATTLESBRIDGE c1955 W195017
The old tide mills at this lowest bridging point of the River Crouch are no longer working, but the spot has developed as a lively antiques centre. The place probably gets its name not from the Battle of Ashington, fought nearby in 1016, but to the Bataille family.

WICKFORD, BROADWAY APPROACH c1960 W195046
Wickford grew around the River Crouch and has since expanded. This view shows shoppers in the town centre, in the days before the 'out of town' shopping centres decimated many such town centres. Note the gentleman with the basket crossing the road.

BURNHAM ON CROUCH, THE RIVER C1965 B325129
The Essex coast is a favourite place for sailors; of all the Essex estuaries, that of the Crouch is generally regarded the best for navigation. This view of the river, thronged with sailing craft, is little changed today.

ALTHORNE, MAIN ROAD C1955 A107005
A classic view of a quiet Essex village, taken in high summer in the 1950s. The village stands above the estuary of the River Crouch, about three miles north west of Burnham-on-Crouch. The Black Lion serves Trumans beers, the well-known firm of London Brewers. Note the 'L' plate on the car.

MALDON, HIGH STREET 1901 46711

A view looking up the remarkably unchanged High Street of this famous and picturesque town situated on a hill above the River Blackwater. The tower in the centre belonged to St Peter's church, the rest of which fell down in 1665. It now houses the magnificent Thomas Plume library, bequeathed to the town in 1704.

LONDON CENTRAL MEAT Co

MALDON, HIGH STREET 1921 70274
The top of Maldon High Street, again little changed. The porchway on the left belongs to the Moot Hall, which was the town hall until 1974 and is now open to the public. In the right foreground, the King's Head still stands, but is no longer an Inn; now, it is the King's Head centre.

MALDON, MARKET HILL 1909 62102
Another period piece, with onlookers watching the photographer working where Market Hill turns sharply to descend to Fullbridge Flow Mill and a bridge over the River Chelmer. The tall house on the left survives, but the cottage on the far right has gone.

MALDON, THE PROMENADE 1909 62098

Here we see Maldon's famous promenade - now Promenade Park - with a fine array of fishing boats; the tower of St Mary's church, with its landmark little white spire, can be seen in the background. Today, the adjacent leisure area has been developed.

MALDON, THE MARINE LAKE 1923 73938

Happy paddlers are at the water's edge. St Mary's church is in the background, and on the right is Maldon's famous Quay, the Hythe. Maldon has been a sailing barge centre for many years; many barges were built here, especially at Cook's Yard, which later maintained the local trading barge fleet.

MALDON, THE RIVER AT BEELEIGH 1906 55547
Here is a vanished sight - a freight barge towed by a horse along the Chelmer and Blackwater Navigation, a scene not dissimilar to those painted by Constable on the Stour Navigation.

HEYBRIDGE, THE BASIN 1903 50231
Across the Blackwater from Maldon, Heybridge is a busy spot. At Heybridge Basin, the Blackwater and Chelmer Navigation looks down into the estuary. Industry, in the form of milling and the Heybridge Iron Works, once flourished here. In later years the Basin was used to moor a collection of barges, which formed the nucleus of the present fleet of the Thames Sailing Barge Club.

FINGRINGHOE, THE CHURCH 1907 57561
Fingringhoe, five miles south of Colchester on the Roman River, was close to a port once used in Roman times, which is now Fingringhoe Wick Nature Reserve. In this view, the ancient St Andrew's church and the church school of 1887 stand together above the pond, fed by a spring seen in the foreground. The spring-water was used by the villagers and sold locally.

GREAT BENTLEY, THE VILLAGE 1902 48290

An evocative view of the inn, the Red Lion, in this little village between Colchester and Clacton. Known for its huge village green, the largest in England, which covers some 42 acres (17 hectares), it is still a place of quiet charms, little changed today.

BRIGHTLINGSEA, SAILING BARGES 1907 57563

The town's nautical connections are clearly seen is this early 20th-century view of the creek, crowded with sailing barges and boats. Famous for its boatyards, which still produce yachts and ships, Brightlingsea is a 'limb' of the Cinque Port of Sandwich, and the Deputy swears allegiance to the mayor of Sandwich.

BRIGHTLINGSEA, HIGH STREET c1955 B209022

Brightlingsea's High Street remains little changed. The town was once famous for its oysters, which were dredged from the creek, but bad weather during the 1950s decimated the industry. On this chilly and windy day, traffic congestion has yet to become a problem in the spacious High Street.

Brightlingsea, High Street c1960 B209023
A view of old Brightlingsea. Only a delivery van disturbs the pedestrians along this part of the High Street, with its quaint mixture of architectural styles. The town was originally situated further inland near the church, but was moved to its present creek-side location during the plague.

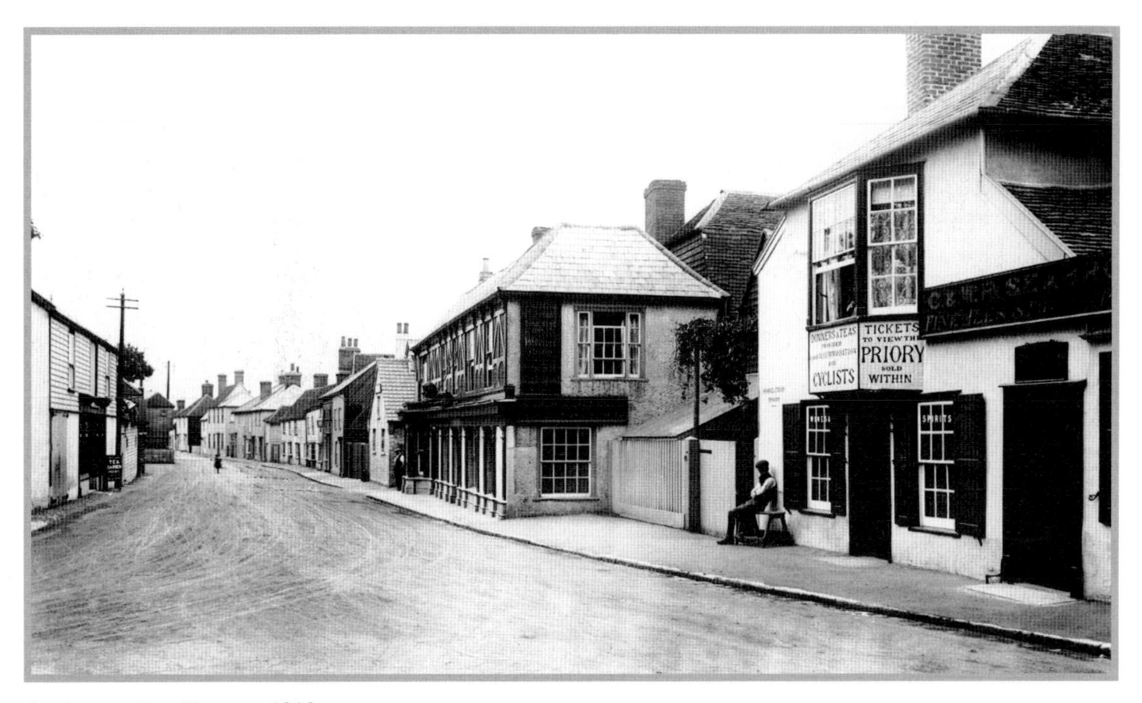

St Osyth, The Village 1912 64263
This isolated village between Clacton-on-Sea and Brightlingsea is famous for its old priory. Little has changed since this photograph was taken save an endless stream of traffic. The Red Lion Inn on the right still exists.

CLACTON-ON-SEA, THE BANDSTAND AND THE PIER 1907 58934
Clacton-on-Sea was founded as a seaside resort in 1871 - the year that the Bank Holiday Act was passed. This view shows the ever popular bandstand and the pier, built in 1873 and lengthened in the 1890s to 1,180ft when the Pavilion was built.

STAND FOR
18

CLACTON-ON-SEA, THE BANDSTAND 1907 58935

In this evocative scene of an English holiday resort, holidaymakers in their deckchairs enjoy the summer sun, facing the sea rather than the bandstand. The bandstand was built in 1899, and military bands played there throughout the season. Clacton was the brainchild of one man - Peter Bruff, an engineer with the Tendring Hundred railway company - who bought 50 acres of farmland here in 1865 with a view to its development as a holiday resort.

CLACTON-ON-SEA, WEST BEACH 1912 64254

Two Thames sailing barges discharge cargo at low water on the beach, whilst drawn higher up are some bathing machines. Horse drawn carts were still used to transport the cargo - probably coal from the north - from the barges. Many of these magnificent flat-bottomed craft were built in Essex.

CLACTON-ON-SEA, PIER GAP 1912 64239
This photograph shows Pier Gap prior to the building of the 'Venetian Bridge'. The shops which lined the steep road down to the pier were demolished shortly after for being 'unhygienic and ugly'. They sold all manner of seaside items from postcards, buckets and spades, paddling shoes and souvenirs to fish and chips, cigarettes and seafood.

CLACTON-ON-SEA, THE BRIDGE 1919 69304
A view of the 'Venetian Bridge' of 1914 and the newly landscaped sides of Pier Gap, laid out by Clacton Council with shrubs and rockery. The shops of the previous picture have disappeared to make way for this 'improvement', an act that now seems to border on vandalism.

CLACTON-ON-SEA, FROM THE JETTY 1912 64252
Clacton was an early promoter of mixed bathing from 1900 onwards, and the town provided unimpeachable arrangements. An array of Mr Cattermole's Bathing Machines is in the centre of the picture. He provided a large assortment of bathing costumes for the ladies. Mr H Norman provided the chairs.

H.NORMAN.

CLACTON-ON-SEA, ELECTRIC PARADE 1913 65239
A fine view of this busy and spacious Clacton street, taken a year before the outbreak of the First World War. Electric Parade was so-called because it was the first part of Clacton to be lit by electricity, but when the novelty wore off, it became, prosaically, part of Pier Avenue.

FRINTON-ON-SEA, CONNAUGHT AVENUE 1921 70307

In the inter-war years Frinton was known for its famous 'summer season' residents, who came for the golf club and the lawn tennis tournament. Gracie Fields once lived in Connaught Avenue in a house called 'Tinkerbell'. This view is little changed today, although the Avenue is no longer almost devoid of traffic.

FRINTON-ON-SEA, CONNAUGHT AVENUE 1921 70308

Connaught Avenue was originally Station Road, but was re-named in Edwardian times when its high-class retail premises earned it the title of 'the Bond Street of East Anglia'. Even today, several old-established shops remain.

Frinton-on-Sea
The Promenade c1955

Frinton was designed and laid out in the late 19th and early 20th centuries by Richard Powell-Cooper as a 'select' seaside resort, full of peace and tranquillity, in direct contrast to brash, noisy, neighbouring Clacton. The famous 'Greensward' stands above the cliffs and the genteel Promenade seen here.

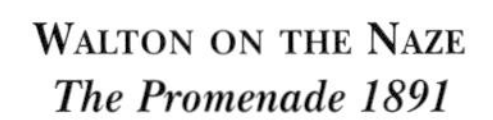

Walton on the Naze
The Promenade 1891

Walton on the Naze was developed as a seaside resort from the early 19th century. After 1855, the town was developed mainly by Peter Bruff, who built Marine Terrace, the central row of houses in this picture. Here families stroll along the parade on the top of the cliffs, which was soon to be developed as Marine Gardens.

Frinton-on-Sea, The Promenade c1955 F53034

Walton on the Naze, The Promenade 1891 29092

WALTON ON THE NAZE, HIGH STREET 1921 70290

A view of the High Street showing - on the left - the Town Hall of 1900, which housed Barclays Bank and the Post Office downstairs. The old Portobello Hotel on the right was built in the 1820s and survived as a hotel for 160 years.

HARWICH, THE QUAYSIDE C1954 H150006

The massive former Great Eastern Hotel, built in 1864, dominates this picture of the quayside. It was built for travellers who came to the Railway Pier to catch the steamers to the continent. It later served as Council Offices, but is now an apartment block.

HARWICH, CHURCH STREET 1954 H150009
A view looking south towards St Nicholas' church of 1821 and the adjoining Three Cups Hotel, part of which dates from the early 16th century. Admiral Nelson and Lady Hamilton stayed there. The 'half-timbered' Wheatsheaf public house on the left dates from the 1920s.

DOVERCOURT, HIGH STREET c1955 D51004
Dovercourt is the seaside neighbour of Harwich, and for many years now has been its shopping centre; Dovercourt was mentioned in Domesday, but Harwich not until the 12th century. The development of the town owes much to John Bagshaw, MP, who died bankrupt in 1800. This bustling view, with Woolworth's on the left, looks towards Kingsway.

East Horndon, Blacksmith Row 1908 60600

The quaint weatherboarded cottages of Blacksmith Row at East Horndon, south of Brentwood, illustrate the quiet rural charm of Essex before the post-war road building programme ripped so many such places to pieces. East Horndon is now almost obliterated by the intersection of the A127 Romford to Southend Road and the A128.

East Horndon, The Boar's Head 1908 60601

Another vanished scene, with chickens foraging for food and children playing by the pond in East Horndon before the hamlet was engulfed by a major cross-roads and roundabout. The brick-built hilltop church is said to be the burial place of the head of Anne Boleyn.

Basildon, Market Place 1961 B438003
A view of the centre of Basildon New Town, the Market Place with its brightly coloured stalls, which was opened in September 1958. This picture shows the booming town centre - up to 1,400 cars were parked there on a Saturday afternoon.

Ingrave, Dairy Farm Pond 1908 60597
Two draught horses are watered at the tree-fringed roadside pond. This picture was taken five years after the composer Vaughan Williams visited Ingrave collecting old folk songs. Here he wrote down 'Bushes and Briars', sung by villagers.

INGRAVE, THE VILLAGE 1908 60599
This view looks northwards along the traffic-free road past the attractive weatherboarded cottages towards Brentwood, some two miles distant. On the right is the truly remarkable red-brick tower of St Nicholas church, built in 1735 by Lord Petre of nearby Thorndon Hall.

BRENTWOOD, THE TOWN HALL 1895 35669
The High Street was not developed in a major way until the 1880s. Boys pose for the camera in the middle of the road, almost devoid of any traffic. The overpowering but rather dull Town Hall, with obligatory clock, dominates the right hand side of the road.

BRENTWOOD, HIGH STREET 1903 50222

A further view of the High Street taken eight years after photograph 35669, this time from closer to the columns of the Town Hall. Little has changed except for the awnings. The White Hart, towards the middle of the picture on the left-hand side, was a Conservative stronghold during the 19th century, while the liberals frequented the nearby Lion & Lamb.

BRENTWOOD, ONGAR ROAD 1907 57578

A delightful scene of urban England in the Edwardian era, reflecting a time of quiet peace that was to be shattered seven years later. The only traffic is bicycles and a horse and cart. In the heat of high summer, the road is dry and dusty.

BRENTWOOD, THE GRAMMAR SCHOOL 1910 62784

The Grammar School was founded in 1558 by Sir Anthony Browne, Lord Chief Justice, and was built on the site of the martyrdom of Thomas Hunter, who was burned at the stake in 1555.

ONGAR, HIGH STREET 1923 74823

Chipping Ongar is so called because of its ancient 'cheaping', or market, and Chipping Ongar is still an important shopping centre. Until recent times, Ongar was the easterly terminus of the Central Line. The town's long High Street is very appealing.

ONGAR, HIGH STREET c1955 O19029
The High Street, looking south, with the King's Head sign on the left. The view is substantially the same today. The shop on the right with an overhang is now an Indian restaurant.

ONGAR, HIGH STREET c1955 O19062
A view looking north along the High Street. The sign for the King's Head Inn is on the right of the picture, although the King's Head itself is in fact on the opposite side of the road standing next to the International Store. The old Town Hall was situated on the right, but was demolished for road widening in 1897 and is now only a memory.

EPPING, HIGH STREET 1921 70132
A busy summer scene on the High Street during the 'roaring twenties', with delivery vans, open-top cars, billowing Union Jack and, on the left, a perambulator with sun awning. A young man is just putting his bicycle into a rack belonging to the tea rooms.

TELEPHONE

EPPING, HIGH STREET 1921 70131

Motorcycles with side-cars wait at the roadside in the broad Epping High Street, little changed today; St John's Church, built in 1888-9 and its tower in 1907, is in the background. The vehicle in the centre of the picture (possibly a motor cycle and sidecar) has proved too fast for the camera.

EPPING, HIGH STREET 1921 70133

A lunchtime view, with Epping's wide High Street and the 1907 tower of St John's church forming the backdrop, of an early London omnibus. The trees were planted in 1887 as part of the Queen Victoria's Golden Jubilee celebrations.

EPPING, HIGH STREET C1955 E38015

Parked cars point the way ahead to congested roads, though little else has changed in this view of Epping High Street. Epping was an important stopping point on the road out of London during the coaching era.

EPPING, CHARCOAL BURNING C1955 E38021

Epping Forest, which now covers some 6,000 acres, was ten times larger in the 17th century. For many years ancient forest crafts were practised, including the making of charcoal from green sticks, which were burned slowly under controlled conditions in great heaps. Two are shown here ready to be covered in turf and fired.

EPPING, VIEW FROM UPSHIRE c1955 E38030

A wonderfully evocative view showing the joys of the motorcar and the open road. A couple in their sporty little number admire the verdant countryside, looking across to Epping Forest from near Waltham Holy Cross, now unfortunately spoiled by the M25.

HARLOW, THE VILLAGE 1903 51086

Before the New Town was even a dream in a developer's eye, a group of children pose for the camera in the quaint little old-world town, with the spire of St Mary the Virgin's Church on the left. This 'village', now known as Old Harlow, is just to the east of the New Town, which was started in 1947 to help relieve London's congestion.

HARLOW, HIGH STREET 1903 51087
Shopkeepers pose at the doors of their premises in this view of the High Street almost a century ago. With the development of the New Town, Harlow's population has mushroomed from a scant 4,000 to over 80,000.

HARLOW, THE FORD 1903 51093
A fine view of a ford which was situated just outside Old Harlow. Fords such as this were once a familiar scene in Essex, but many have now gone, including this one, a victim of new roadbuilding associated with the New Town.

ROYDON, THE MILL c1955 R229016

ROYDON
The Mill c1955
Roydon Mill still stands on the River Stort close to the border with Hertfordshire. Nearby are the ruins of Nether Hill, where Sir Thomas More courted his wife in the early 16th century.

ROYDON
The Village c1900
A cycling club gathers under a patriotic banner for a group picture, possibly during the Diamond Jubilee celebrations of 1897. Some of the bicycles appear to be decorated with garlands.

ROYDON, THE VILLAGE c1900 R229306B

NAZEING, THE POND c1955 N66003

Nazeing is perched on the hills above the Lea valley a few miles south-west of Harlow. It sports a big breezy common, which is actually private property, and a pond. Nazeing is known for the former Lea valley glasshouse industry.

WALTHAM ABBEY, OLD TEMPLE BAR 1906 55213

Just over the border in Hertfordshire stands the west entrance to Theobalds Park, actually Old Temple Bar, which stood in Fleet Street, London, until 1888. It was designed by Sir Christopher Wren and erected in 1672. Heads of executed prisoners used to be exposed on it.

WALTHAM ABBEY, HIGHBRIDGE STREET 1921 70159
A wonderful view of Waltham Abbey in the inter-war years. This view looks up Highbridge Street from the river bridge to the Abbey church and its impressive 16th-century west tower. The M25 now skirts the south of this former market town, and link roads have destroyed some of the town's ancient character and streets.

WALTHAM ABBEY, THE TOWN HALL AND HIGHBRIDGE STREET 1921 70160
The Town Hall stands on the left of this photograph, which was taken from outside the church and looking down Highbridge Street. Of interest are the vans on the right advertising a 'Scenic Railway'; perhaps they were part of a summer fair?

WALTHAM ABBEY, THE GATEWAY c1955 W14003
An unusual view of the Abbey Gateway - in the centre - and the bridge over the Cornmill Stream, a tributary of the River Lea, with people relaxing around the broken walls. A modern link road now runs through the background to this picture.

WALTHAM ABBEY, THE CHURCH C1955 W14004

Waltham Abbey Church was the nave of the former Abbey church and was saved as the parish church at the Dissolution. The tower collapsed in 1552 and the bells were sold to pay for the repairs. The new bells are some of the most renowned in England and inspired Tennyson's poem 'Ring out wild bells!'

WALTHAM ABBEY, SUN STREET C1955 W14010

A post-war view of one of the old narrow streets of Waltham, this time Sun Street, which ran east from the Market Square. Three old houses in the street now accommodate Epping Forest District Museum.

WALTHAM ABBEY, THE OLD ABBEY GATEWAY C1955 W14022
A picture of the Old Abbey Gateway, which leads to the Abbey Gardens and the Lee Valley Park Countryside Centre. The abbey is associated with King Harold - he who was killed at Hastings - who paid for its rebuilding in 1057. An Augustinian monastery was founded here in 1177.

CHIGWELL, THE VILLAGE C1955 C88006
Chigwell, situated on the edge of Hainault forest, has been much developed over the years, but the village still presents a deceptively leafy appearance. The bakery and tea-rooms are reminders that many Londoners came on country outings to Chigwell, either by bus or by the Central Line tube.

INGATESTONE, HIGH STREET 1925 78741

A banner across the road advertises the July flower show on a virtually deserted High Street. The High Street - on the line of the Romans' great road into East Anglia - is known for its pleasing mixture of 16th- and 17th-century Georgian houses. A motorcycle is parked outside the Police Station.

BLACKMORE, THE VILLAGE c1955 B320009

BLACKMORE
The Village c1955

This quiet village is tucked away in the Essex lanes about four miles north of Brentwood. It is chiefly known for its 15th-century church belfry, constructed in timber in three stages. The shop is still the hub of the village, but the man on his bike and the lack of traffic speak of a now bygone age.

CHELMSFORD
The Shire Hall 1892

Chelmsford, the county town of Essex, was founded by the Romans and inhabited by the Saxons, but its growth was slow, not really developing until the 19th and 20th centuries. The centre around Tindal Square, dominated by the civilised Shire Hall built between 1789 and 1791, remains unspoiled.

CHELMSFORD, THE SHIRE HALL 1892 31507

CHELMSFORD, DUKE STREET 1906 56883

Duke Street has changed much since this picture was taken in Edwardian days; the photograph itself records a great change from the early Victorian era, when the original Fair Ground in Duke Street was first built over. Today, Duke Street is known for its office blocks, estate agents and building societies.

CHELMSFORD, DUKE STREET 1919 69017

Here we see a busy scene, with parked cars on the right and an open-topped bus bound for Southend chugging down the Street on the left. The picture is taken from close to the railway bridge, looking towards Tindal Square. The chimney belongs to the Wells and Perry brewery.

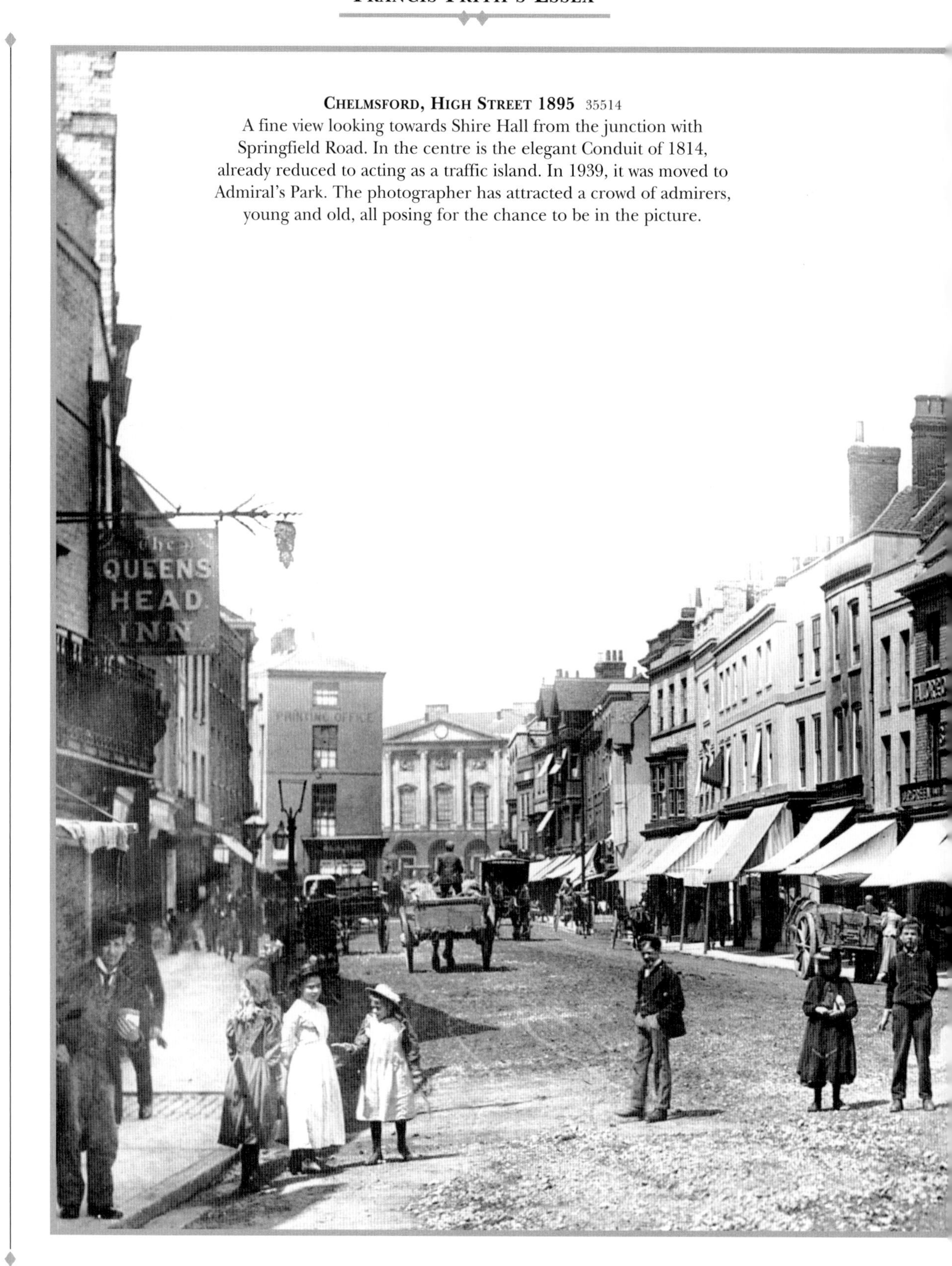

CHELMSFORD, HIGH STREET 1895 35514
A fine view looking towards Shire Hall from the junction with Springfield Road. In the centre is the elegant Conduit of 1814, already reduced to acting as a traffic island. In 1939, it was moved to Admiral's Park. The photographer has attracted a crowd of admirers, young and old, all posing for the chance to be in the picture.

IPSWICH
BOOT
&
SHOE
WAREHOUSE
IPSWICH
HIGH ST
BARNARD UPHOLSTERER

CHELMSFORD, HIGH STREET 1898 41504

Three years after photograph 35514, a photographer returned; once again a crowd of children pose in front of the Conduit. The Conduit stood originally in Tindal Square above a spring known as Burgess Well, but was moved to the junction of Springfield Road and High Street in 1852. In the three years between the two photos, the Ipswich Boot and Shoe Warehouse has given way to Barnards, cabinet maker, upholsterer and decorator.

BARNARDS
HOTEL
BARNARD
CABINET MAKER
UPHOLSTERER
&
DECORATOR

CHELMSFORD, HIGH STREET 1919 69011

A view looking back down High Street to the Conduit, with the King's Head - one of Chelmsford's old inns - just behind it in the centre. Woolworth's has long occupied the site, and the High Street is now completely pedestrianised. On the right is Bolingbroke and Sons, a well-known Chelmsford department store.

CHELMSFORD, MOULSHAM STREET 1919 69019

This is an action-packed picture crowded with bicycles, pedestrians and prams. During the Middle Ages, Moulsham was a separate village from Chelmsford. On the left is Rankin's, a well-known draper's shop, and between them and the Regent Theatre is Hawke's confectioners.

CHELMSFORD, MOULSHAM STREET 1919 69020
Several timber buildings still survive in this street, which is a continuation of the High Street. Unfortunately, the building on the right, known as 'The Friars', was demolished in the 1930s. The Parkway now crosses Moulsham Street at this point.

DANBURY, THE VILLAGE 1903 50235
Danbury is situated on the main road between Chelmsford and Maldon. Danbury Hill is the second highest point in Essex, and the old village spreads downhill from this point. Sir Walter Scott mentioned the 16th-century Griffin Inn, which still stands, in his 'Waverley' novels.

HATFIELD PEVEREL, THE POST OFFICE C1965 H173016

This view looks eastwards along the former Roman road to Colchester, which forms the main street of this village. The church, whose spire can be seen, is the Methodist church.

LEXDEN, THE VILLAGE 1904 52361

Lexden was once a little village a few miles to the west of Colchester, but has now been subsumed as a suburb. This 1904 view shows the village pub and the then brand-new tramway, which ran out from Colchester to terminate here. The trams were replaced by buses in December 1929.

WITHAM, HIGH STREET 1900 46225
Witham's High Street - Newland Street - lies along the Roman road to Colchester, later to be the Great Essex turnpike. The Spread Eagle and the White Hart - two important stopping places for a change of horses - are on the left of the picture.

WITHAM, HIGH STREET 1900 46223
Another turn-of-the-century view of Newland Street, looking towards the Collingwood Road junction, bustling with pedestrians. A few onlookers, including two dogs, watch the photographer at work.

WITHAM, CHIPPING HILL 1900 46240
This was the original settlement at Witham and still retains its village atmosphere. The name comes from the old word for 'market', and the nearby Woolpack Inn recalls the main merchandise. This view is taken from the green. The village smithy was at the back of the overhanging house on the left.

KELVEDON, HIGH STREET 1925 78735
We are looking west towards the termination of the High Street at the Old Convent - a view virtually unchanged today. Kelvedon lies on the site of the Roman town of Canonium, about midway between Chelmsford and Colchester.

KELVEDON, HIGH STREET 1925 78736

This view looks east along the High Street, which lies on the Roman road between London and Colchester. High Street is rich in pleasing architecture, and the scene is little changed today. Kelvedon was the birthplace of Charles Haddon Spurgeon, the great Baptist preacher, son of a Kelvedon minister.

COLCHESTER, NORTH HILL 1891 28211

North Hill descends from the High Street. The church on the right is St Peter's - the town church. The tower was completed in 1758. In 1878 the Victorian clock was regulated by Greenwich time so as to agree with the clock at the Post Office. On the left is William Robert Simkin's shop. He was cabinet-maker, chair maker and upholsterer, as well as undertaker.

CHEMIST
AND
DRUGGIST
SURGEON DENTIST
LONDON
JOSLIN
IRONMONGER

COLCHESTER, HIGH STREET 1892 31518
Looking east along High Street, which was dominated by the spire of Sir Giles Gilbert Scott's church of St Nicholas and St Runwald. This replaced two older churches (St Runwalds and St Nicholas), but was itself demolished in 1955 and replaced by a parade of shops, known as St Nicholas House. The tower of All Saints' church is visible in the background.

COLCHESTER, HEAD STREET 1891 28212

This view looks north along Head Street, towards North Hill. This has always been an important part of commercial Colchester. Shops include the premises of William Frederick Allen, tailor and woollen draper, Henry Aggso, piano manufacturers and Mattacks, booksellers.

COLCHESTER, THE CASTLE 1892 31524

Colchester Castle - the largest Norman Keep ever built - stands on the site of the Roman temple of Claudius, which was destroyed during the Boudiccan rebellion of AD60. Today it houses the Castle Museum. This picture shows the castle prior to the excavation of the outer walls in the 1930s, and the castle entrance is now reached across a footbridge.

COLCHESTER, ST BOTOLPH'S PRIORY 1892 31528
A classic picture of the Priory. Re-used Roman bricks and tiles went into the building of St Botolph's priory church; it is still an impressive ruin today, although it is divested of its mantling of vegetation. This was the first Augustinian house in England.

COLCHESTER, HIGH STREET AND TOWN HALL 1901 47650
A busy late morning scene in Colchester's High Street at the turn of the century. The Town Hall, which dominates this view, was not completed until 1902. The High Street lies along the central axis of the Roman legionary fortress, which was built here in AD43. The scene is not greatly changed today.

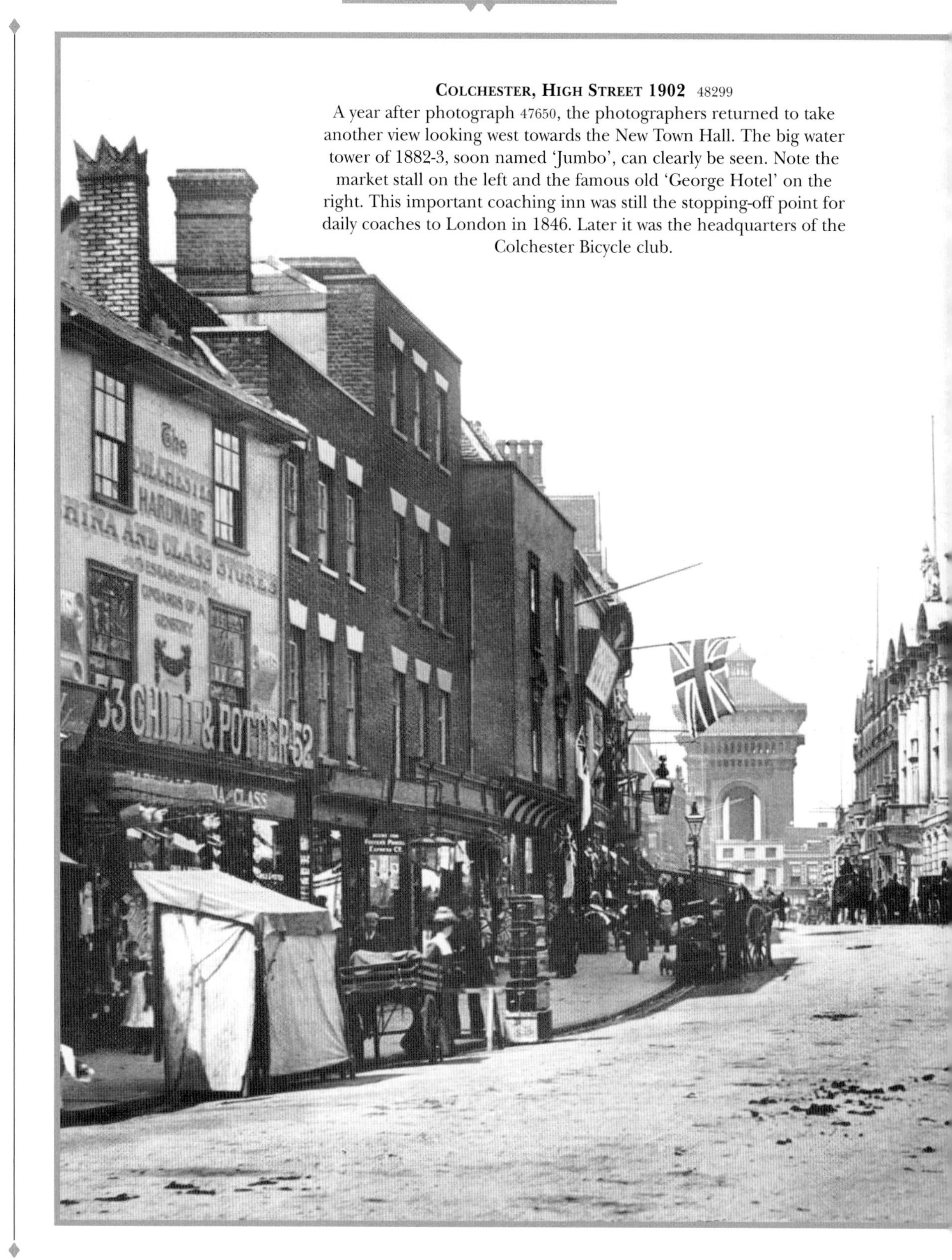

COLCHESTER, HIGH STREET 1902 48299

A year after photograph 47650, the photographers returned to take another view looking west towards the New Town Hall. The big water tower of 1882-3, soon named 'Jumbo', can clearly be seen. Note the market stall on the left and the famous old 'George Hotel' on the right. This important coaching inn was still the stopping-off point for daily coaches to London in 1846. Later it was the headquarters of the Colchester Bicycle club.

GEORGE HOTEL
GEORGE HOTEL

COLCHESTER, VINEYARD STREET 1904 52348

Vineyard Street was christened in about 1854, named after a supposed vineyard in this vicinity. This picture is taken outside the Brewer's Arms, associated with the nearby brewery of Thomas Osborne. To the left is St John's Street - formerly known as 'Gutter Lane' from the open gutter which ran along it. Gorham the bootmaker's shop is on the middle left, while a group pose outside Hales Dairy; Stridd's grocery store is on the far left.

COLCHESTER, STOCKWELL STREET 1904 52349

Situated in the Dutch Quarter, where Flemings settled, Stockwell Street still has some good medieval houses. The gabled Stockwell Arms seen opposite still exists - in 1866 the bellringers of St Peter's church ate a good supper here, having rung one thousand changes on St Peter's church bells. Opposite is the swinging sign of another inn - the Nelson's Head.

COLCHESTER, PARK LANE 1921 70369

A view of part of Castle Park, created in 1892-3 as a public park. When Lower Castle Park, seen here, was opened in 1893, this lake was still unfinished. The building to the left of the centre is Chippings Mill, one of at least four mills that formerly served Colchester.

12 E.C.WAT N. 12
AND AT
TO LET
TO LET
TELEGRAPH OFFICE
POST OFFICE

Saffron Walden, The Post Office 1912 65087
Saffron Walden is named after the plant, saffron, which was used for dyeing woollen cloth here in the Middle Ages, when the town was prosperous and important in the wool trade.

SAFFRON WALDEN, HIGH STREET 1919 69134
A car passes up the High Street, while a horse-drawn conveyance comes down the hill. Wright's Garage, on the right, emphasises that shortly after the First World War the internal combustion engine had begun to supersede the railways. The half-timbered building is the Cross Keys. The Post Office, opposite, is still at the same early 18th-century premises.

TO THE
Ford
SERVICE DEPOT
10 KING ST PHONE 62
34 WALKER

SAFFRON WALDEN, MARKET PLACE 1932 85111
The Market Place is predominantly Victorian and is the second 'centre' of the lovely old town - the High Street is the first. It is little changed architecturally from when this picture was taken.

DEBDEN, THE CROSS ROADS C1955 D89002
A nostalgic rural scene, taken in days when it was still safe to walk a pram beside the road. This shows the cross-roads of Water Lane and Debden Road, between Debden and Saffron Walden, looking towards Debden. It is little changed from this view today, and the milestone on the left still stands.

GREAT SAMPFORD, CHURCH CORNER c1955 G91006

Great Sampford is a pleasant village in northern Essex on the road between Finchingfield and Saffron Walden. It is little changed today, with these attractive gabled houses near the lovely old 14th-century church of St Michael, built by the Knights Hospitallers.

THAXTED, THE OLD GUILDHALL 1906 55458

This is one of the most famous buildings in Essex, situated in what was, during the 14th and 15th centuries, one of its most prosperous towns. This view is little changed today, dominated by the magnificent Guildhall, built in the 15th century for the cutlers of Thaxted.

GREAT EASTON, THE FORD 1951 G95001
Here we see a vanished scene. Two draught horses are led over the old bridge by the ford on the river Chelmer. The photographer appears to have left his car parked up the road on the left and walked back down over the river to capture this timeless view.

DUNMOW, HIGH STREET c1955 D90002
The Saracen's Head - on the right of this picture - was a famous coaching inn at Great Dunmow, a town associated since 1949 with the Dunmow Flitch ceremony. This had originated at Little Dunmow in 1140 and fallen into neglect in 1751. Every four years a side of bacon (a flitch) is presented to a married couple who can prove that they have not regretted their marriage a year and a day after the ceremony.

FINCHINGFIELD, THE VILLAGE 1903 50569
A less familiar view of this much-photographed place. Finchingfield, about seven miles north west of Braintree, with its wide green and pond on the River Pant, remains little changed today. This view of the pond and ducks looks away from the famous windmill and church.

CASTLE HEDINGHAM, THE VILLAGE C1955 C238001
This lovely little town was granted its Charter in the 13th century. It is remarkably unspoiled and little changed from when this picture was taken. The Castle is one of Essex's two great medieval fortresses; it was built during King Stephen's reign by Aubrey de Vere, whose father had fought at Hastings. His descendants, the Earls of Oxford, held it for 550 years.

RAYNE, THE VILLAGE 1901 46725

Rayne is still a charming village with a long history, little changed from this photograph. All the buildings shown still exist, though the Post Office Stores is now the Tandoori Cottage Restaurant.

BLACK NOTLEY, THE VILLAGE 1909 62127

Black Notley is a little village just to the south of Braintree. This photograph shows a tranquil scene, with a horse taking refreshment at the former mill pond. The mill stands next to the pub, the Reindeer, which still stands. This is the birthplace of John Ray, a fellow of Trinity College, Cambridge, who wrote the first definitive 'History of Plants'.

BLACK NOTLEY, THE VILLAGE 1909 62128

A further view of this peaceful little village, this time looking the other way past the pub and the mill to the village. The only things that moved too fast for the photographer on this summer's day were the ducks by the pond on the left.

CRESSING, THE VILLAGE 1909 62124
Villagers pose for the camera outside their homes in this little village near Braintree. This was the earliest English settlement of the Knights Templar, who were given the manor in 1135. Cressing is known today for its medieval barns at nearby Cressing Temple.

BRAINTREE, MARKET SQUARE 1900 46244
George Courtauld MP presented the fountain, which still stands, to the town in 1882. On market days, this open area would be full of wagons and stalls as well as penned livestock. Today, such market scenes have almost entirely vanished.

BOCKING, BRADFORD STREET 1902 48279

Bocking is now a suburb of Braintree. This view shows picturesque Bradford Street, which winds down the hill towards the River Blackwater and Bradford Bridge. Today, this is a conservation area, and many of these fine buildings are listed.

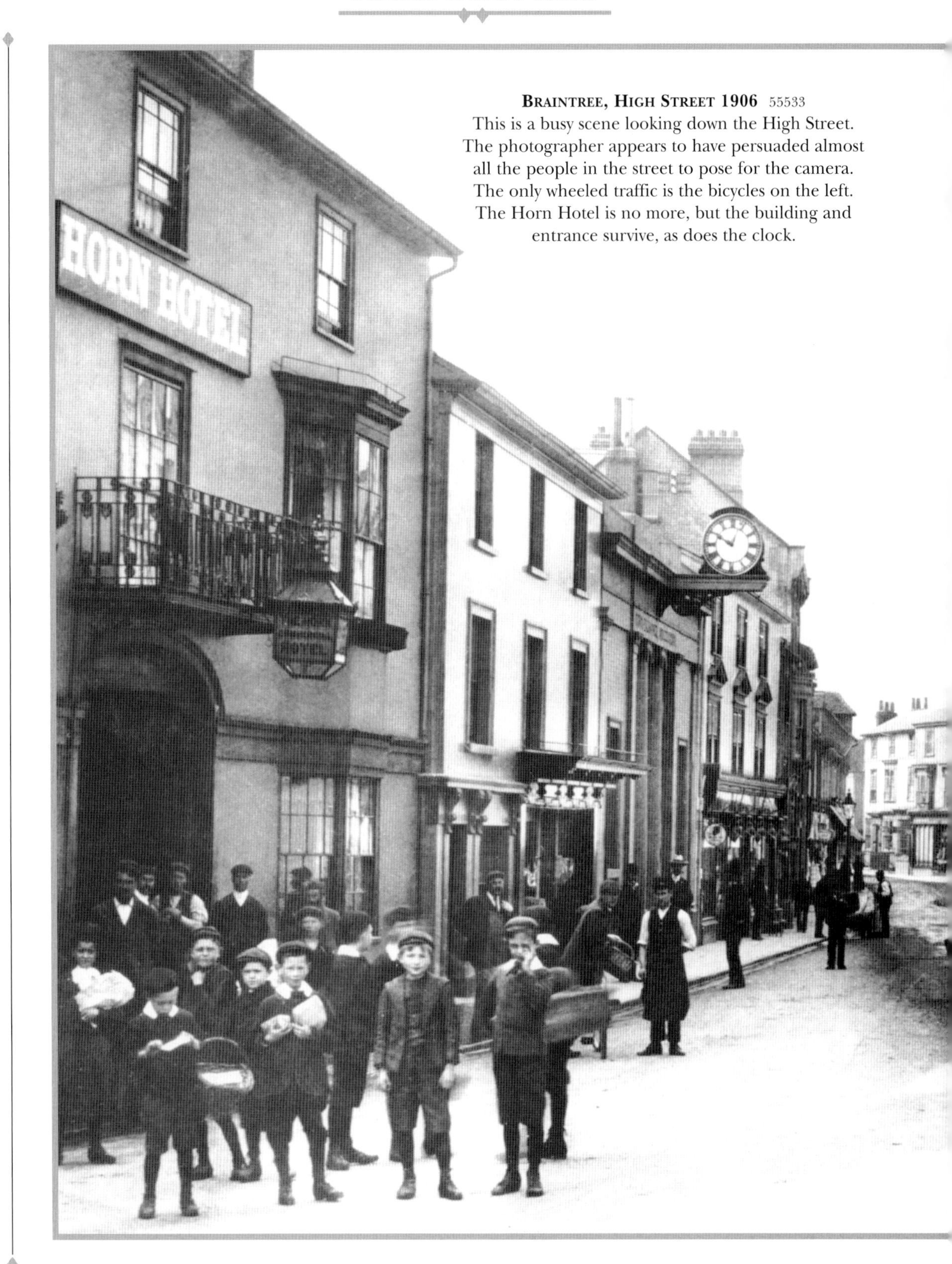

BRAINTREE, HIGH STREET 1906 55533
This is a busy scene looking down the High Street. The photographer appears to have persuaded almost all the people in the street to pose for the camera. The only wheeled traffic is the bicycles on the left. The Horn Hotel is no more, but the building and entrance survive, as does the clock.

ESSEX
AND
SUFFOLK
FIRE
OFFICE

HALSTEAD, HIGH STREET 1952 H168010
This town, which stands above the Colne in the north of the county about five miles from Braintree, was once famous for its silk and crepe. This wonderful post-war view looks up the High Street, with a motorbike and sidecar parked in the foreground.

HALSTEAD, HIGH STREET c1955 H168011
A view looking downhill along the wide High Street, lined with small country-style shops, towards the River Colne. The scene is almost unchanged today; only the cars and fashions give away that the picture was taken nearly fifty years ago.

BURES, HIGH STREET C1955 B324004

A delightful picture of Bures, a pleasing collection of villages which straddle the river Stour and the county boundary with Suffolk. This picture shows the type of architecture so common hereabouts, although these particular buildings are just over the border into Suffolk. The photographer has also caught two boys playing on a pedal cycle.

COGGESHALL, STONEHAM STREET C1965 C242056

Here we see the pretty centre of Coggeshall, an attractive village now given over to the antiques trade. It was once a prosperous wool town, and famed for its lace. Little has changed since this picture was taken, save that the clock tower of 1887 is now painted blue and white.

COGGESHALL
East Street c1955

Vernacular Essex architecture is seen to good effect in this picture of East Street, a continuation of West Street along the line of the old Roman Road, the Essex Stane Street - once the main A120, but now by-passed. The scene has changed little, but the town has become more self-conscious since this picture was taken.

MATCHING GREEN
The Pond 1960

The pond is a haven for wildlife as well as a happy place for anglers and is little changed today. The village, a few miles to the east of Harlow, is known for its Marriage Feast Room, which dates from the 15th century; this is a large upper floor room designed for weddings.

MATCHING GREEN, THE POND 1960 M128013

Index

Frith Book Co Titles

www.francisfrith.co.uk

The Frith Book Company publishes over 100 new titles each year. A selection of those currently available are listed below. For latest catalogue please contact Frith Book Co.
Town Books 96 pages, approximately 100 photos. ***County and Themed Books*** 128 pages, approximately 150 photos (unless specified). All titles hardback with laminated case and jacket, except those indicated pb (paperback)

Amersham, Chesham & Rickmansworth (pb)	1-85937-340-2	£9.99
Andover (pb)	1-85937-292-9	£9.99
Aylesbury (pb)	1-85937-227-9	£9.99
Barnstaple (pb)	1-85937-300-3	£9.99
Basildon Living Memories (pb)	1-85937-515-4	£9.99
Bath (pb)	1-85937-419-0	£9.99
Bedford (pb)	1-85937-205-8	£9.99
Bedfordshire Living Memories	1-85937-513-8	£14.99
Belfast (pb)	1-85937-303-8	£9.99
Berkshire (pb)	1-85937-191-4	£9.99
Berkshire Churches	1-85937-170-1	£17.99
Berkshire Living Memories	1-85937-332-1	£14.99
Black Country	1-85937-497-2	£12.99
Blackpool (pb)	1-85937-393-3	£9.99
Bognor Regis (pb)	1-85937-431-x	£9.99
Bournemouth (pb)	1-85937-545-6	£9.99
Bradford (pb)	1-85937-204-x	£9.99
Bridgend (pb)	1-85937-386-0	£7.99
Bridgwater (pb)	1-85937-305-4	£9.99
Bridport (pb)	1-85937-327-5	£9.99
Brighton (pb)	1-85937-192-2	£8.99
Bristol (pb)	1-85937-264-3	£9.99
British Life A Century Ago (pb)	1-85937-213-9	£9.99
Buckinghamshire (pb)	1-85937-200-7	£9.99
Camberley (pb)	1-85937-222-8	£9.99
Cambridge (pb)	1-85937-422-0	£9.99
Cambridgeshire (pb)	1-85937-420-4	£9.99
Cambridgeshire Villages	1-85937-523-5	£14.99
Canals And Waterways (pb)	1-85937-291-0	£9.99
Canterbury Cathedral (pb)	1-85937-179-5	£9.99
Cardiff (pb)	1-85937-093-4	£9.99
Carmarthenshire (pb)	1-85937-604-5	£9.99
Chelmsford (pb)	1-85937-310-0	£9.99
Cheltenham (pb)	1-85937-095-0	£9.99
Cheshire (pb)	1-85937-271-6	£9.99
Chester (pb)	1-85937-382 8	£9.99
Chesterfield (pb)	1-85937-378-x	£9.99
Chichester (pb)	1-85937-228-7	£9.99
Churches of East Cornwall (pb)	1-85937-249-x	£9.99
Churches of Hampshire (pb)	1-85937-207-4	£9.99
Cinque Ports & Two Ancient Towns	1-85937-492-1	£14.99
Colchester (pb)	1-85937-188-4	£8.99
Cornwall (pb)	1-85937-229-5	£9.99
Cornwall Living Memories	1-85937-248-1	£14.99
Cotswolds (pb)	1-85937-230-9	£9.99
Cotswolds Living Memories	1-85937-255-4	£14.99
County Durham (pb)	1-85937-398-4	£9.99
Croydon Living Memories (pb)	1-85937-162-0	£9.99
Cumbria (pb)	1-85937-621-5	£9.99
Derby (pb)	1-85937-367-4	£9.99
Derbyshire (pb)	1-85937-196-5	£9.99
Derbyshire Living Memories	1-85937-330-5	£14.99
Devon (pb)	1-85937-297-x	£9.99
Devon Churches (pb)	1-85937-250-3	£9.99
Dorchester (pb)	1-85937-307-0	£9.99
Dorset (pb)	1-85937-269-4	£9.99
Dorset Coast (pb)	1-85937-299-6	£9.99
Dorset Living Memories (pb)	1-85937-584-7	£9.99
Down the Severn (pb)	1-85937-560-x	£9.99
Down The Thames (pb)	1-85937-278-3	£9.99
Down the Trent	1-85937-311-9	£14.99
East Anglia (pb)	1-85937-265-1	£9.99
East Grinstead (pb)	1-85937-138-8	£9.99
East London	1-85937-080-2	£14.99
East Sussex (pb)	1-85937-606-1	£9.99
Eastbourne (pb)	1-85937-399-2	£9.99
Edinburgh (pb)	1-85937-193-0	£8.99
England In The 1880s	1-85937-331-3	£17.99
Essex - Second Selection	1-85937-456-5	£14.99
Essex (pb)	1-85937-270-8	£9.99
Essex Coast	1-85937-342-9	£14.99
Essex Living Memories	1-85937-490-5	£14.99
Exeter	1-85937-539-1	£9.99
Exmoor (pb)	1-85937-608-8	£9.99
Falmouth (pb)	1-85937-594-4	£9.99
Folkestone (pb)	1-85937-124-8	£9.99
Frome (pb)	1-85937-317-8	£9.99
Glamorgan	1-85937-488-3	£14.99
Glasgow (pb)	1-85937-190-6	£9.99
Glastonbury (pb)	1-85937-338-0	£7.99
Gloucester (pb)	1-85937-232-5	£9.99
Gloucestershire (pb)	1-85937-561-8	£9.99
Great Yarmouth (pb)	1-85937-426-3	£9.99
Greater Manchester (pb)	1-85937-266-x	£9.99
Guildford (pb)	1-85937-410-7	£9.99
Hampshire (pb)	1-85937-279-1	£9.99
Harrogate (pb)	1-85937-423-9	£9.99
Hastings and Bexhill (pb)	1-85937-131-0	£9.99
Heart of Lancashire (pb)	1-85937-197-3	£9.99
Helston (pb)	1-85937-214-7	£9.99
Hereford (pb)	1-85937-175-2	£9.99
Herefordshire (pb)	1-85937-567-7	£9.99
Herefordshire Living Memories	1-85937-514-6	£14.99
Hertfordshire (pb)	1-85937-247-3	£9.99
Horsham (pb)	1-85937-432-8	£9.99
Humberside (pb)	1-85937-605-3	£9.99
Hythe, Romney Marsh, Ashford (pb)	1-85937-256-2	£9.99
Ipswich (pb)	1-85937-424-7	£9.99
Isle of Man (pb)	1-85937-268-6	£9.99
Isle of Wight (pb)	1-85937-429-8	£9.99
Isle of Wight Living Memories	1-85937-304-6	£14.99
Kent (pb)	1-85937-189-2	£9.99
Kent Living Memories(pb)	1-85937-401-8	£9.99
Kings Lynn (pb)	1-85937-334-8	£9.99

Available from your local bookshop or from the publisher

Frith Book Co Titles (continued)

Lake District (pb)	1-85937-275-9	£9.99
Lancashire Living Memories	1-85937-335-6	£14.99
Lancaster, Morecambe, Heysham (pb)	1-85937-233-3	£9.99
Leeds (pb)	1-85937-202-3	£9.99
Leicester (pb)	1-85937-381-x	£9.99
Leicestershire & Rutland Living Memories	1-85937-500-6	£12.99
Leicestershire (pb)	1-85937-185-x	£9.99
Lighthouses	1-85937-257-0	£9.99
Lincoln (pb)	1-85937-380-1	£9.99
Lincolnshire (pb)	1-85937-433-6	£9.99
Liverpool and Merseyside (pb)	1-85937-234-1	£9.99
London (pb)	1-85937-183-3	£9.99
London Living Memories	1-85937-454-9	£14.99
Ludlow (pb)	1-85937-176-0	£9.99
Luton (pb)	1-85937-235-x	£9.99
Maidenhead (pb)	1-85937-339-9	£9.99
Maidstone (pb)	1-85937-391-7	£9.99
Manchester (pb)	1-85937-198-1	£9.99
Marlborough (pb)	1-85937-336-4	£9.99
Middlesex	1-85937-158-2	£14.99
Monmouthshire	1-85937-532-4	£14.99
New Forest (pb)	1-85937-390-9	£9.99
Newark (pb)	1-85937-366-6	£9.99
Newport, Wales (pb)	1-85937-258-9	£9.99
Newquay (pb)	1-85937-421-2	£9.99
Norfolk (pb)	1-85937-195-7	£9.99
Norfolk Broads	1-85937-486-7	£14.99
Norfolk Living Memories (pb)	1-85937-402-6	£9.99
North Buckinghamshire	1-85937-626-6	£14.99
North Devon Living Memories	1-85937-261-9	£14.99
North Hertfordshire	1-85937-547-2	£14.99
North London (pb)	1-85937-403-4	£9.99
North Somerset	1-85937-302-x	£14.99
North Wales (pb)	1-85937-298-8	£9.99
North Yorkshire (pb)	1-85937-236-8	£9.99
Northamptonshire Living Memories	1-85937-529-4	£14.99
Northamptonshire	1-85937-150-7	£14.99
Northumberland Tyne & Wear (pb)	1-85937-281-3	£9.99
Northumberland	1-85937-522-7	£14.99
Norwich (pb)	1-85937-194-9	£8.99
Nottingham (pb)	1-85937-324-0	£9.99
Nottinghamshire (pb)	1-85937-187-6	£9.99
Oxford (pb)	1-85937-411-5	£9.99
Oxfordshire (pb)	1-85937-430-1	£9.99
Oxfordshire Living Memories	1-85937-525-1	£14.99
Paignton (pb)	1-85937-374-7	£7.99
Peak District (pb)	1-85937-280-5	£9.99
Pembrokeshire	1-85937-262-7	£14.99
Penzance (pb)	1-85937-595-2	£9.99
Peterborough (pb)	1-85937-219-8	£9.99
Picturesque Harbours	1-85937-208-2	£14.99
Piers	1-85937-237-6	£17.99
Plymouth (pb)	1-85937-389-5	£9.99
Poole & Sandbanks (pb)	1-85937-251-1	£9.99
Preston (pb)	1-85937-212-0	£9.99
Reading (pb)	1-85937-238-4	£9.99
Redhill to Reigate (pb)	1-85937-596-0	£9.99
Ringwood (pb)	1-85937-384-4	£7.99
Romford (pb)	1-85937-319-4	£9.99
Royal Tunbridge Wells (pb)	1-85937-504-9	£9.99
Salisbury (pb)	1-85937-239-2	£9.99
Scarborough (pb)	1-85937-379-8	£9.99
Sevenoaks and Tonbridge (pb)	1-85937-392-5	£9.99
Sheffield & South Yorks (pb)	1-85937-267-8	£9.99
Sherborne (pb)	1-85937-301-1	£9.99
Shrewsbury (pb)	1-85937-325-9	£9.99
Shropshire (pb)	1-85937-326-7	£9.99
Shropshire Living Memories	1-85937-643-6	£14.99
Somerset	1-85937-153-1	£14.99
South Devon Coast	1-85937-107-8	£14.99
South Devon Living Memories (pb)	1-85937-609-6	£9.99
South East London (pb)	1-85937-263-5	£9.99
South Somerset	1-85937-318-6	£14.99
South Wales	1-85937-519-7	£14.99
Southampton (pb)	1-85937-427-1	£9.99
Southend (pb)	1-85937-313-5	£9.99
Southport (pb)	1-85937-425-5	£9.99
St Albans (pb)	1-85937-341-0	£9.99
St Ives (pb)	1-85937-415-8	£9.99
Stafford Living Memories (pb)	1-85937-503-0	£9.99
Staffordshire (pb)	1-85937-308-9	£9.99
Stourbridge (pb)	1-85937-530-8	£9.99
Stratford upon Avon (pb)	1-85937-388-7	£9.99
Suffolk (pb)	1-85937-221-x	£9.99
Suffolk Coast (pb)	1-85937-610-x	£9.99
Surrey (pb)	1-85937-240-6	£9.99
Surrey Living Memories	1-85937-328-3	£14.99
Sussex (pb)	1-85937-184-1	£9.99
Sutton (pb)	1-85937-337-2	£9.99
Swansea (pb)	1-85937-167-1	£9.99
Taunton (pb)	1-85937-314-3	£9.99
Tees Valley & Cleveland (pb)	1-85937-623-1	£9.99
Teignmouth (pb)	1-85937-370-4	£7.99
Thanet (pb)	1-85937-116-7	£9.99
Tiverton (pb)	1-85937-178-7	£9.99
Torbay (pb)	1-85937-597-9	£9.99
Truro (pb)	1-85937-598-7	£9.99
Victorian & Edwardian Dorset	1-85937-254-6	£14.99
Victorian & Edwardian Kent (pb)	1-85937-624-X	£9.99
Victorian & Edwardian Maritime Album (pb)	1-85937-622-3	£9.99
Victorian and Edwardian Sussex (pb)	1-85937-625-8	£9.99
Villages of Devon (pb)	1-85937-293-7	£9.99
Villages of Kent (pb)	1-85937-294-5	£9.99
Villages of Sussex (pb)	1-85937-295-3	£9.99
Warrington (pb)	1-85937-507-3	£9.99
Warwick (pb)	1-85937-518-9	£9.99
Warwickshire (pb)	1-85937-203-1	£9.99
Welsh Castles (pb)	1-85937-322-4	£9.99
West Midlands (pb)	1-85937-289-9	£9.99
West Sussex (pb)	1-85937-607-x	£9.99
West Yorkshire (pb)	1-85937-201-5	£9.99
Weston Super Mare (pb)	1-85937-306-2	£9.99
Weymouth (pb)	1-85937-209-0	£9.99
Wiltshire (pb)	1-85937-277-5	£9.99
Wiltshire Churches (pb)	1-85937-171-x	£9.99
Wiltshire Living Memories (pb)	1-85937-396-8	£9.99
Winchester (pb)	1-85937-428-x	£9.99
Windsor (pb)	1-85937-333-x	£9.99
Wokingham & Bracknell (pb)	1-85937-329-1	£9.99
Woodbridge (pb)	1-85937-498-0	£9.99
Worcester (pb)	1-85937-165-5	£9.99
Worcestershire Living Memories	1-85937-489-1	£14.99
Worcestershire	1-85937-152-3	£14.99
York (pb)	1-85937-199-x	£9.99
Yorkshire (pb)	1-85937-186-8	£9.99
Yorkshire Coastal Memories	1-85937-506-5	£14.99
Yorkshire Dales	1-85937-502-2	£14.99
Yorkshire Living Memories (pb)	1-85937-397-6	£9.99

See Frith books on the internet www.francisfrith.co.uk

Frith Products & Services

Francis Frith would doubtless be pleased to know that the pioneering publishing venture he started in 1860 still continues today. A hundred and forty years later, The Francis Frith Collection continues in the same innovative tradition and is now one of the foremost publishers of vintage photographs in the world. Some of the current activities include:

Interior Decoration

Today Frith's photographs can be seen framed and as giant wall murals in thousands of pubs, restaurants, hotels, banks, retail stores and other public buildings throughout the country. In every case they enhance the unique local atmosphere of the places they depict and provide reminders of gentler days in an increasingly busy and frenetic world.

Product Promotions

Frith products are used by many major companies to promote the sales of their own products or to reinforce their own history and heritage. Frith promotions have been used by Hovis bread, Courage beers, Scots Porage Oats, Colman's mustard, Cadbury's foods, Mellow Birds coffee, Dunhill pipe tobacco, Guinness, and Bulmer's Cider.

Genealogy and Family History

As the interest in family history and roots grows world-wide, more and more people are turning to Frith's photographs of Great Britain for images of the towns, villages and streets where their ancestors lived; and, of course, photographs of the churches and chapels where their ancestors were christened, married and buried are an essential part of every genealogy tree and family album.

Frith Products

All Frith photographs are available Framed or just as Mounted Prints and Posters (size 23 x 16 inches). These may be ordered from the address below. From time to time other products - Address Books, Calendars, Table Mats, etc - are available.

The Internet

Already fifty thousand Frith photographs can be viewed and purchased on the internet through the Frith websites and a myriad of partner sites.

For more detailed information on Frith companies and products, look at these sites:

www.francisfrith.co.uk
www.francisfrith.com
(for North American visitors)

See the complete list of Frith Books at:

www.francisfrith.co.uk

This web site is regularly updated with the latest list of publications from the Frith Book Company. If you wish to buy books relating to another part of the country that your local bookshop does not stock, you may purchase on-line.

For further information, trade, or author enquiries please contact us at the address below:

The Francis Frith Collection, Frith's Barn, Teffont, Salisbury, Wiltshire, England SP3 5QP.

Tel: +44 (0)1722 716 376 Fax: +44 (0)1722 716 881 Email: sales@francisfrith.co.uk

See Frith books on the internet at www.francisfrith.co.uk

FREE PRINT OF YOUR CHOICE

Mounted Print
Overall size 14 x 11 inches (355 x 280mm)

Choose any Frith photograph in this book. Simply complete the Voucher opposite and return it with your remittance for £3.50 (to cover postage and handling) and we will print the photograph of your choice in SEPIA (size 11 x 8 inches) and supply it in a cream mount with a burgundy rule line (overall size 14 x 11 inches). **Please note**: aerial photographs and **photographs with a reference number starting with a "Z" are not Frith photographs and cannot be supplied under this offer. Offer valid for delivery to one UK address only**.

***PLUS:* Order additional Mounted Prints at HALF PRICE - £9.50 each** (normally £19.00)
If you would like to order more Frith prints from this book, possibly as gifts for friends and family, you can buy them at half price (with no additional postage and handling costs).

***PLUS:* Have your Mounted Prints framed**
For an extra £18.00 per print you can have your mounted print(s) framed in an elegant polished wood and gilt moulding, overall size 16 x 13 inches (no additional postage and handling required).

IMPORTANT!

These special prices are only available if you use this form to order. You must use the ORIGINAL VOUCHER on this page (no copies permitted). We can only despatch to one UK address. This offer cannot be combined with any other offer.

Send completed Voucher form to:
The Francis Frith Collection, Frith's Barn, Teffont, Salisbury, Wiltshire SP3 5QP

CHOOSE A PHOTOGRAPH FROM THIS BOOK

*for **FREE** and Reduced Price Frith Prints*

Please do not photocopy this voucher. Only the original is valid, so please fill it in, cut it out and return it to us with your order.

Picture ref no	Page no	Qty	Mounted @ £9.50	Framed + £18.00	Total Cost £
		1	Free of charge*	£	£
			£9.50	£	£
			£9.50	£	£
			£9.50	£	£
			£9.50	£	£
			£9.50	£	£
			* Post & handling		£3.50
			Total Order Cost		£

Please allow 28 days for delivery. Offer available to one UK address only

Title of this book ....
I enclose a cheque/postal order for £ ....
made payable to 'The Francis Frith Collection'

OR please debit my Mastercard / Visa / Maestro card, details below

Card Number

Issue No (Maestro only) Valid from (Maestro)

Expires Signature

Name Mr/Mrs/Ms ....
Address ....
....
....
.... Postcode ....
Daytime Tel No ....
Email ....

Valid to 31/12/12

Free Print - see overleaf

Would you like to find out more about Francis Frith?

We have recently recruited some entertaining speakers who are happy to visit local groups, clubs and societies to give an illustrated talk documenting Frith's travels and photographs. If you are a member of such a group and are interested in hosting a presentation, we would love to hear from you.

Our speakers bring with them a small selection of our local town and county books, together with sample prints. They are happy to take orders. A small proportion of the order value is donated to the group who have hosted the presentation. The talks are therefore an excellent way of fundraising for small groups and societies.

Can you help us with information about any of the Frith photographs in this book?

We are gradually compiling an historical record for each of the photographs in the Frith archive. It is always fascinating to find out the names of the people shown in the pictures, as well as insights into the shops, buildings and other features depicted.

If you recognize anyone in the photographs in this book, or if you have information not already included in the author's caption, do let us know. We would love to hear from you, and will try to publish it in future books or articles.

Our production team

Frith books are produced by a small dedicated team at offices in the converted Grade II listed 18th-century barn at Teffont near Salisbury, illustrated above. Most have worked with the Frith Collection for many years. All have in common one quality: they have a passion for the Frith Collection. The team is constantly expanding, but currently includes:

Jason Buck, John Buck, Douglas Burns, Ruth Butler, Heather Crisp, Isobel Hall, Hazel Heaton, Peter Horne, James Kinnear, Tina Leary, Sue Molloy, Hannah Marsh, Kate Rotondetto, Dean Scource, Eliza Sackett, Terence Sackett, Sandra Sanger, Lewis Taylor, and Shelley Tolcher.